Independent Schools
Examinations Board

English Practice Exercises 11+
Answer Book

Andrew Hammond

Editor: Ann Entwisle

Independent Schools
Examinations Board

www.galorepark.co.uk

GALORE PARK

Published by ISEB Publications, an imprint of Galore Park Publishing Ltd
19/21 Sayers Lane, Tenterden, Kent TN30 6BW
www.galorepark.co.uk

Printed by Replika Press, India

ISBN: 978 1 907047 84 8

First published 2012

Details of other ISEB publications and examination papers, and Galore Park
publications are available at www.galorepark.co.uk

Contents

Part one: Comprehension

Exercise 1.1: *Brave Pilot* from *Battle of Britain* by Chris Priestley

Question	Answer	Mark	Additional guidance
1.	He is referring to the sensation of leaving earth behind and soaring into the sky.	1	
2.	*Answers should refer to:* • literal descriptions of nature: orchards, hedgerows in blossom, hop fields all suggest vibrant colours in Britain • darker colours in France, through similes such as 'soot-black skies of Dunkirk' • dramatic metaphors such as 'a huge wall of black smoke' and 'filthy cloak'	4	Reward references to *how* language is used – i.e. similes, metaphors – as well as actual quotations from passage. Look for contrasts in bright/dark colours either side of Channel.
3.	The previous paragraph showed writer's sense of relief, good news, everything okay – no danger – so this is unexpected.	2	
4.	An awareness that something or someone is behind you (without seeing them).	2	Any sensible explanation of being aware beyond our usual sensory perception.
5.	*Answers may include references to:* • ships and wrecks everywhere • studded with men all waiting to escape • like a 'Biblical' scene – with thousands of people waiting for deliverance	3	More than one feature/description is needed. Reward special reference to Biblical scene.
6.	Could see evidence of the destruction caused by their attacks – bombsites and damaged ships and buildings	2	

7.	*Any sensible examples, including:* • 'Behind you!… Behind who? Behind who?' (creates a sense of panic in cockpit) • 'screaming, screaming, and screaming') more panic and fear	2	Full marks for one example *and* an explanation of its effect on the reader.
8.	The long sentence describes the gentle landscape back home – slower-paced, relaxed. Shorter sentences later on create a more urgent, frantic feeling. The author may be attempting to reflect the tension inside the cockpit, creating excitement for the reader, and developing empathy for the character.	4	
9.	*Answers may refer to:* • romantic – sensitive to feelings of flying, and attractive landscape below • brave to be flying off to war • modest/lacking confidence in own ability • nervous, twitchy under pressure	5	Reward opinions justified by evidence from the passage; two statements, with two examples; bonus 5th mark available for eloquent, insightful answers (must relate to **character** rather than appearance/mood etc.)

Exercise 1.2: *The Charioteer of Delphi* by Caroline Lawrence

Question	Answer	Mark	Additional guidance
1.	*Answers may vary, for example:* Nubia felt like she was floating in the vast expanse of space around her – bouncing around on the chariot was like being on water.	2	1 mark for a less clear/complete explanation.
2.	Nubia struggles to hear his words over the 'thunder of nearly two hundred hooves'.	1	
3.	'To her right were tier upon tier of empty seats not yet illuminated by the sun.'	1	
4.	*Answers may include:* • 'a line of pounding horses stretching away to her left and right.' • 'nearly two hundred hooves'	1	
5.	*Possible evidence includes:* • 'Here he tipped his body to the left …' • 'Urbanus's whole body moved as he drove …' • 'even bending forward at the waist to urge on the horses.' • 'He was leaning so far forward at the waist that his body was horizontal …'	2	Full marks for a pertinent quotation and concise explanation.
6.	*Look for references to:* • Nubia relies on him for safety: 'Nubia screamed and clutched Urbanus's waist …' • Nubia is impressed by his skill: 'he gave a deft tug of the innermost rein with his left hand. Nubia gasped as they took the turn.'	3	Any sensible answer with some reference to the passage – either literal or inferred.
7.	*Answers may include:* Driven, determined person: • 'every iota of his being was focused on his horses and the track ahead.' Nimble, athletic and strong: • 'But he came down as nimbly as an acrobat …'; • 'stiff and awkward on land, but behind a team of four stallions Scopas was as lithe as a dancer.'	3	Look for references to more than one aspect of this character (i.e. personality *and* skill).

8. (a)	*Answers may include:* • 'Nubia screamed and clutched Urbanus's waist' • 'Nubia gasped as they took the turn.' • Urbanus tells Nubia what is happening throughout, and what their objective is.	3	Reward answers which include specific references to what is happening in the passage and/or specific quotations.
(b)	*Answers may include:* • he knows what he is doing • he is able to control the chariot and the horses well • 'Urbanus's whole body moved as he drove, leaning first one way, then the other, even bending forward at the waist to urge on the horses.'	3	
9.	*Answers may include:* • continuous, fast-paced action: 'Then the wheels bit sand and then they were bouncing down the straight again.' • reaction of Nubia: ' Nubia screamed and clutched Urbanus's waist'; 'Nubia closed her eyes for half a circuit and held tight...'; 'Nubia gasped' • references to senses: e.g. 'above the thunder of nearly two hundred hooves' • powerful verbs: e.g. 'exploded out of the stalls' and 'Nubia screamed' • similes and metaphors: 'like plunging into a pool of water' • example of long/short sentences for effect: e.g. lines 26–28	6	Reward answers that give a range of evidence from the text and discuss different techniques used.

5

Exercise 1.3: *The Myth of the Mountainfolk* from *Cloudsailors* by Hugh Montgomery

Question	Answer	Mark	Additional guidance
1.	*Answers may vary; ideas include:* • creates a more affectionate feel – evoking reader's affections • more vulnerable, delicate • link to mother nature – giving birth to Man	2	
2.	'But they were one people, and would travel from high to low, low to high, sharing the wealth of root and berry, never taking more from the Earth than she could afford to give.'	1	
3.(a)	'as the ivy grows inseparable from the branches of the ageing oak.'	1	
(b)	It emphasises how closely the people were tied to their landscape. It links well with the theme of Nature.	2	Two marks for two points, including the link to Nature, or for one point well explained.
4.	The Lowlanders found the air to be sparse and thin in the Mountains so they travelled there less frequently, and eventually they were unable to ascend at all.	2	
5.	*Answers may include:* • resilient to the harsh mountain air – growing accustomed to the harshness... • thin and delicate people, disliking the heavy vapours of the lowlands • eventually unable to withstand the lowland air • shy and gentle people	2	Two marks for two different observations.

6.(a)	They found the air to be too heavy and it caused them to cough after spending a short while there.	2	
(b)	They built coracles of ice and used them to sail across to other peaks where they found food ('bounty').		
7.	Answers may include: • 'Their cities grew, consuming everything around them.' • 'Trees were felled, whole forests cleared.' • 'Fumes and phosphor filled the air, thickening to a distant smear of yellow paste above the towns.' • 'Before long the valley air became acrid..'	2	Two marks for two different quotations – both demonstrating the Lowlanders' lack of respect for the Earth.
8.	Answers may include: • 'In the beginning, far, far in the distant past...' – use of chronological phrases here – a classic opening to a myth or legend • 'the Earth was born.' – personification of the Earth – powerful metaphors, in keeping with mythical style • 'Amidst this beauty dwelled the Menfolk.' – use of the words 'amidst' and 'dwelled' provides a traditional style; 'Menfolk' rather than 'humans' is more mythical	4	Look for relevant quotations and an explanation of the effects of each one – i.e. creating a mythical feel/traditional story-telling language.
9.	Answers will vary	5	Reward comments that show understanding of the relationship between the two races, and of the different ways they treat the landscape.

Exercise 1.4: *A Dragon's Diet* from *Dragon Boy* by Dick King Smith

Question	Answer	Mark	Additional guidance
1.	The tinned knight which he had eaten the night before caused the belching.	1	
2.(a)	A knight might taste metallic due to his armour.	1	
(b)	Montagu does not enjoy eating knights: 'It's not that I really like the taste of the fellows...'.	1	
3.	A person with a will made of 'iron' is very strong minded. Iron is used metaphorically, as it is a very strong metal.	2	Full marks for a clear explanation.
4.	Mrs Bunsen-Burner would not be pleased to be told this, for dragons take pride in the ugliness of their appearance, not the beauty.	2	Only one mark for a 'no' answer without an explanation.
5.	Mrs Bunsen-Burner's attitude towards her husband at the beginning seems bossy and in control: '..it was seldom that he summoned up the courage to oppose her will which was of iron.' After he has paid her a compliment, however, her 'blood-red eyes softened' and 'she would have fluttered her eyelashes if she had had any.'	3	Full marks for a clear explanation.
6.	*Answers may vary; look for references to:* • he often belches, but he apologises afterwards (plus quote to support); • he dislikes eating knights, but does so because they are pests (plus quote to support); • he can usually be found snoozing in the forest and minding his own business (plus quote to support); • he is clever enough to be able to get what he wants by using flattery (plus quote to support).	3	Three marks for several points and explanations.

7.	*Answers will vary; look for references to:* • use of humour throughout • view of dragons is opposite to traditional view (i.e. humorous and inoffensive, rather than fire-breathing and ferocious) • viewing knights from the dragon's point of view, rather than the other way round • use of modern, informal words and phrases throughout, rather than traditional language of myths and legends	3	Full marks for insightful observations and explanations.
8.	*Answers may vary and may include:* • comical portrayal of Mr Bunsen-Burner as affable and polite: 'I do beg your pardon, my dear.' • suggestion that dragons are sleepy, inoffensive creatures: 'I was having a snooze in the forest, minding my own business, harming neither man nor beast...'	4	Four marks for two good points with explanations and evidence in support.
9.	*Answers will vary:* Look for a recognition of style, content and theme. Pupils should begin by developing the issue of Mr Bunsen's diet.	5	

Exercise 1.5: *A Surprise Visit* from *Blitzcat* by Robert Westall

Question	Answer	Mark	Additional guidance
1.	*Answers may refer to:* • 'cat limping' • 'she looked thin, beaten, furtive'	1	
2.(a)	'He had no feelings about cats one way or another.'	1	
(b)	*Answers could refer to:* This cat was 'an event in the monotony.' – she provided a distraction in an otherwise tedious day.	2	
3.	*Answers will vary; look for references to:* • low self esteem • little regard for what he can achieve • unable to do the simplest of tasks	2	Full marks for clear explanation with reference to the words in the quotation in the question.
4.	The cat fled at first but then leapt up onto the sandbags beside him and began purring wildly, rubbing herself against his hand to show affection.	2	More than one action for full marks.
5.	*Answers may include:* • he became happy/merry/carefree; • he felt happier with himself for doing someone a good turn •	2	Full marks for a clear explanation.
6.	*Possible words are:* • post • sandbags • garrison • war in France •	2	Only half marks for less subject-specific words – e.g. binoculars
7.	*Answers will vary, and may include references to:* • on patrol (e.g. for the Home Guard) • at a lookout post • on sentry duty	3	Full marks for a clear, sensible suggestion, based on evidence in the passage.

8.	*Answers may refer to the following evidence:* • '...this terrifying world,...' • his mental state – low self esteem, lack of confidence (through fear) • 'his fear made him feel slightly sick all the time.' • 'The blood seemed to move in his veins for the first time in a fortnight.'	4	Four marks for a full explanation with evidence from the passage.
9.	Look for accurate portrayal of the man, based on his behaviour and thoughts in the passage. Look also for wife's character coming through (e.g. 'Janet told him off when he brought back his sandwiches uneaten.')	6	

Exercise 1.6: *The Giant Under the Snow* by John Gordon

Question	Answer	Mark	Additional guidance
1.	*Answers will vary and may include references to:* • builds tension • arouses curiosity • makes the reader wonder what is surrounding Jonk • by leaving out any detail it builds suspense • what is *not* said can be just as effective as what *is* said	2	Full marks for comment and explanation or expansion.
2.	The copse is made up of several ridges splaying out from a low flattish mound – four straight ones and one shorter, bent one, like the fingers of a hand.	2	Full marks for a full explanation. One mark only for a partial explanation.
3.	• 'The horn bleated again…' • 'nagging like Mrs Stevens.'	2	One mark for including the second quote only. (The first phrase is the preferred option).
4.	Jonk stooped to brush her coat and saw it shining on the ground where she had disturbed the soil when she jumped from the mound.	2	
5.	Jonk thought it might have been a clutch of worms wintering under the soil.	2	
6.	*Look for references to:* • observant: notices the way the mound is built up • a vivid imagination: 'A hand? What if it closed on her!'; 'Her imagination was trying to frighten her…' • determined: '…she would not be beaten.' • resilient: ' a moment later she crawled clear unhurt.' • short tempered: 'a sudden spurt of anger…' • cautious at times: 'she paused'; 'But she was afraid.'	3	Full marks for three observations with some evidence in support.
7.	Jonk leaves the copse in fear when the ground appears to ripple beneath the surface, without cracking, and a strange sigh is heard. The giant hand appears to be coming to life.	3	Full marks for a full explanation. Two or one mark for incomplete/unclear comments.

8.	*Answers will vary. Look for reference to the descriptions in the passage. Examples may include:* • a religious building – large temple, its ruins now covered in grass • an ancient sculpture – perhaps of a giant lying down • a burial ground • a sleeping giant	4	Reward answers which reflect the clues and descriptions provided in the passage.
9.	*Answers may include:* Use of personification throughout: • references to 'gigantic hand' • 'between the fingers' • 'The green hand had given her a gift.' • 'It no longer seemed unfriendly.' Suggestion of movement and sound: • A ripple ran the length of the ridge.' • 'with a soft sound almost like a sigh from underground,' • 'it humped itself in the middle.' The reactions of Jonk: • unsettling questions asked, e.g. 'A hand? What if it closed on her!' • 'It seemed to clutch at her and she almost cried out.' • 'But she was afraid.'	5	Reward clear observations supported by pertinent evidence from the passage.

Exercise 1.7: *Greek Heroes* by Geraldine McCaughrean

Question	Answer	Mark	Additional guidance
1.	The Race of Gold were a vain and proud race.	2	
2.	*Answers could include:* • 'he used gold' • 'of course he did' • 'buffed up to a shine'	2	Reward insightful comments and relevant quotations.
3.	The Race of Silver did not prance about and flaunt their beauty. They were not as proud a race as their ancestors of gold.	2	
4.	'Ghostly loveliness' suggests a shimmering, elusive quality – as though the silver shimmers like a transparent, ghostly apparition.	3	Reward clear explanations, which make the connection between the silver and a ghostly apparition. Two or one marks for incomplete or unclear comments.
5.	*Answers will vary and may include references to:* bronze is: functional, industrial, industrious, very strong The Race of Bronze certainly lived up to its name. Its people were: • 'tireless and hardworking' • 'brutally strong' • it built forges	3	Reward full explanations supported by clear evidence from the passage.
6.	*Answers will vary. Look for sensible comments which may refer to:* • some humans can be proud and vain • some can be inactive and lazy • others can be hard working but obsessed with war • building humans requires care and effort – not just special materials • humans require managing/controlling	3	Reward any sensible, insightful comments.
7.	'He lavished the tenderest care on his little manikins and grew fond of them, for all their imperfections.'	2	One mark for a less appropriate or incomplete sentence.

8.	*Answers will vary and may include references to:* • by using precious metals, Zeus hoped the humans would be a fine race • Zeus hoped he would be feel proud of his new creation • he had high expectations for them	3	
9.	*Examples include:* • 'prance and preen and pride themselves': this emphasizes their delicate, soft and precious character – 'p' is a soft consonant • 'elegant and effete': again, 'e' is a soft-sounding consonant, suggesting delicate, refined race • 'sinuous, silvery': poetical, attractive sound, increases their appeal • 'brazen bones': a hard sounding consonant which reflects the hard, brash Race of Bronze	4	Two accurate examples of alliteration supported by comments about their effectiveness, for full marks.

Exercise 1.8: *A Visitor to Stay* from *Heidi* by Joahanna Spyri

Question	Answer	Mark	Additional guidance
1.	The old man did not appear to recognise Heidi, as it says he was 'staring searchingly' at her.	2	
2.	Her aunt.	1	
3.	• Heidi is pleased to see the old man. • 'She went straight up to him and held out her hand.'	2	
4.	The old man's look suggested that he was very angry with Peter, so he decided it was best to leave at once.	2	Full marks for a clear, sensible explanation, showing evidence of understanding of the passage.
5.	That is for you to cope with. That is your business now.	2	
6.	Detie does not feel comfortable about leaving Heidi with the old man, as it says in the passage, 'Detie was really far from easy in her mind about what she was doing...'	3	Reward sensible, clear answers with good evidence in support. Fewer marks for incomplete explanations of less relevant quotations.
7.	Detie is able to make her views known and defend herself to her Uncle. She says, 'Now it's your turn,' and '...that's your affair,' for example. But she is also wary of her Uncle: 'She was quite frightened by the way he looked at her, and took a few steps backward.'	3	Full marks for a balanced explanation and good evidence in support.
8.	*Answers may vary. Look for references to:* • a stern manner: 'he exclaimed gruffly'; 'he demanded roughly' • an old man: 'with his long beard and bushy grey eyebrows' • quite bossy towards Peter: 'And you be off with your goats' • short tempered: 'snapped the old man' • he must be caring because he is still willing to take her	4	Reward any insightful comments and observations, with relevant evidence in support.

9.	Letters will vary. Look for references to how Detie regards her Uncle, how she feels he will react to this new visitor and why she feels it is his turn to care for Heidi now.	6	Reward sensitive writing in character as Detie, showing empathy for her position and knowledge of the circumstances as revealed in the passage.

Exercise 1.9: *Moving House* from *Millions* by Frank Cottrell Boyce

Question	Answer	Mark	Additional guidance
1.	From Damien's viewpoint.	1	
2.	*Answers will vary. A possible answer:* The word 'architectural' relates to the design of the house, and it is this aspect that does not impress Damien. He uses the term architectural because it fits with the previous paragraph – written by would-be estate agent, Anthony.	3	Reward clear, sensible explanations, relating directly to the passage.
3.	Before the houses were built the fields were sectioned off using string, to mark each plot, so the writer is referring to the area of land which was demarked to become the Cromarty Close estate.	3	Reward accurate explanations of the purpose of the string – i.e. the metaphor 'made of string' is not to be taken literally.
4.	Dogger, Finisterre and Cromarty are all street names – or will become street names when the estate is built.	1	
5.	The misunderstanding arose when Damien thought his father meant that they were to live in the field of string – i.e. with no houses in it – and it is this which appealed to Damien, hence his enthusiastic, 'Yes, please!'	2	
6.	When he first visited the site, the area was a field of brambles with string lines to demark where the plots lay. When he returned the brambles and string had gone and there was now an exclusive housing estate marked 'Portland Meadows', made up of four rows (or streets) of houses with pointy roofs and funny shaped windows.	4	Full marks for clear, detailed descriptions of the site before *and* after the housing estate had been constructed. Two marks for each part.
7.	St Simeon lived alone on top of a tall column so he could avoid the temptations of the world. Distracted by sightseers, he moved to an even higher column.	3	

8.(a)	We moved there.	1	
(b)	*Answers may vary. Look for:* • it makes it seem like a simple decision, though it must have been a major one for the family • it creates an almost comical / light hearted effect, contributing to the tone of the passage • it emphasizes the child-like quality of the narration – told simply by Damien	3	Reward answers which make more than one point about the effect of the short paragraph.
9.	*Answers may include:* • Anthony uses words and phrases which are well-known estate agents' terms, and unusual for a boy to use, e.g. property, cost-efficient, en suite, semi-rural • Anthony refers to the cost of the house and says that it will 'retain its value well or most likely go up' – it is unusual for a ten/eleven year old to be interested in the housing market	5	Look for detailed explanations supported by close reference to the passage. Fewer marks for less detailed explanations and little or no evidence in support.

Exercise 1.10: *A Sleeping Passenger* from *Night Birds on Nantucket* by Joan Aiken

Question	Answer	Mark	Additional guidance
1.	It was her breathing which prevented her from resembling a wax doll.	1	
2.	'…gravely watching over her.'	2	
3.	*Answers may vary; look for references to:* • dramatic effect • highlights extraordinary fact, i.e. to sleep for ten months • greater impact on reader • for emphasis	2	Reward accurate and sensible explanations of the author's intentions / effect on the reader. One mark for brief/ incomplete explanations.
4.	Nate	1	
5.	*Answers may include:* • Why don't you cease caring for her? • Why don't you stop looking after her? • Why don't you give up?	2	
6.	The girl may have brought them good luck because they now have as much whale oil as they can hold.	2	
7.	*Answers may vary. Acceptable descriptions include:* • shifty looking • with a gaunt face • rude • unsympathetic/uncaring • disrespectful	3	One mark for each reasonable word or phrase. Three separate descriptions needed for full marks. Own words required.
8.	*Answers may vary. Acceptable descriptions include:* • caring: 'as he carefully raised the child..' • altruistic/considerate/selfless: 'whenever he had any time to spare he chose to spend it by the sleeping child' • resilient: 'taking no notice of these remarks' • supportive: 'Come on now, young 'un,…'	4	Reward insightful, observant comments which are each supported by relevant evidence from the passage. Two descriptions with two pieces of evidence will do.

9.	*Answers will vary. Look for references to the setting, conditions, atmosphere and language used.*	5	The more successful responses will reflect the style and atmosphere of the original passage. The continuations need to lead on from this stage in the story and refer to events and characters from the passage.

Exercise 1.11: *The Dark Forest* from *Shadowmancer* by G. P. Taylor

Question	Answer	Mark	Additional guidance
1.	Beadle was startled when a deer bolted from a holly bush and ran deeper into the forest.	1	No marks for a fox.
2.	Beadle would rather spend the night by the fireside in the inn, listening to stories and drinking warm beer.	2	One mark for an incomplete answer.
3.	*Possible answer:* The simile 'like a dark blanket' suggests that the thulak can smother their victims, shutting off all light and plunging them into darkness.	2	
4.	*Answers will vary, and may include the following quotations:* • 'Beadle feared the thulak more than anything' • 'He could hardly say the words' • 'he whispered feebly' • 'whispered the now terrified Beadle'	3	Three separate words or phrases for full marks. Reward any other sensible quotation found.
5.	The Parson is not frightened of the thulak. *Evidence includes:* • he asks Beadle, 'What are you frightened of? • he shouts their name three times • he says, 'I fear nothing and no one, and they have every reason in the world to fear me.'	2	Reward any sensible answer with supporting evidence. No marks for suggesting that the Parson is frightened of the thulak.
6.	*Answers will vary. A possible answer:* '... my mother said that I should beware of them, for they can steal up on you at night and rob you of your will to live. They are the most fearsome creatures of the forest.'	3	Reward interesting, empathetic answers that accurately refer back to Beadle's earlier thoughts on the thulak.
7.	*Answers will vary; look for interesting, insightful comments and theories, based on evidence presented in the passage.*	2	

8.	Answers may vary. Accept any sensible thoughts and impressions which allude to the master/servant or guardian/charge nature of the relationship and include some or all of the following evidence: • 'timidly following a tall, confident man' • '(he) clutched at the cloaked figure that he followed so closely' • 'and hide inside his companion's cloak' • 'Beadle hunched his shoulders and buried his face in the musty black cloak of his tall, angry companion' • 'Demurral towered over the cowering, frightened form of his servant'	4	
9.	Answers will vary. Look for references to the setting, conditions, atmosphere and language used.	5	The more successful responses will reflect the style and atmosphere of the original passage. The continuations need to lead on from this stage in the story and refer to events and characters from the passage.

23

Exercise 1.12: *Tell Me No Lies* by Malorie Blackman

Question	Answer	Mark	Additional guidance
1.	Her mother's scarf, which is decorated with moons and stars, is draped across Gemma's lamp, causing these shapes to be projected onto her ceiling.	2	
2.	*Answers may vary. Possible alternatives for dark and mysterious (in the passage) include:* • strange • moody • magical • mystical • gloomy/shaded	2	One mark for each synonym offered. Or two marks for a complete phrase.
3.	Gemma keeps photographs of mothers/mums in her scrapbook.	1	
4.	*Either:* A mother rescues a child from an overturned car. *Or:* A mother does not give up hope for her ill son and, after he is refused the necessary treatment in Britain, she takes him to America, where he gets a heart and liver transplant and survives.	1	
5.(a)	*Possible responses are:* • Gemma likes (and craves) happy endings • Gemma is obsessive • Gemma needs love (from a mother) • Gemma is lonely and in need of comfort/reassurance	2	Two separate points for two marks, or one point, fully explained.
(b)	*Possible responses are:* • Taiwan is argumentative/ persistent • Taiwan is disrespectful to his father • Taiwan does not like listening to his father • Taiwan likes to defend himself/stick up for himself	2	Two separate points for two marks, or one point, fully explained.

6.	*Sentences may include the following descriptions:* Gemma's room is: • safe • secure • magical • mystical • peaceful • like a fantasy world Downstairs is: • noisy • filled with conflict • real life • stressful • unsettling	3	Reward insightful observations which reflect accurate reading and understanding of the passage. Up to three sentences needed for full marks – i.e. one for Gemma's room and two for downstairs (or the reverse).
7.	*Accept either:* 'Tarwin and Dad were at it again.' *Or:* 'Every evening they had a shouting match, a contest to see who could raise the roof first.'	2	
8.	*Answers will vary; accept anything sensible and related to the evidence in the passage, for example:* Gemma may collect photographs of other heroic mums because her own mother may be absent from her life. Perhaps she has died or has moved away. Gemma's fondness of 'happy endings' may reflect some sadness in her own life.	4	Reward sensible, empathetic responses, supported by relevant evidence from the passage.
9.(a)	*Answers will vary.*	2	Reward thoughtful responses, which relate to the passage.
(b)	*Answers will vary. Look for (and reward) understanding – and demonstration – of how the author's use of language has impacted on the reader – i.e. specific words and phrases from the passage and a note about their effect.*	4	Two marks for two examples of language used, and two marks for two explanations / commentaries.

Exercise 1.13: *The Snow Goose* by Paul Gallico

Question	Answer	Mark	Additional guidance
1.	*A possible answer:* The author means a wild and desolate place, still relatively undisturbed by human inhabitation.	2	
2.	*Answers may vary; possible responses include:* The word 'restless' implies that the sea is: • always moving to and fro • never constant • fluctuating/changing form • tidal	2	Reward sensible, insightful explanations for the choice/meaning of the word and a comment on its effectiveness.
3.	• tidal creeks • estuaries • small rivers	2	Any two will do.
4.	*Acceptable answers include:* • defence • barricade • protection • safeguard	1	Accept definitions which relate to this particular context.
5.	It was used again recently as a home for someone.	2	Reward answers which replace each key word from the passage.
6.	The story may have gained its title from the 'great white bird with the black-tipped pinions that saw it all from the beginning to the end'.	2	
7.	*Answers may include references to:* • the depiction of a harsh landscape in which Rhayader has to survive: 'It is desolate, utterly lonely...' • the description of him as a 'lonely man' • the description of his 'warped' and 'ugly' appearance but of his capacity to create 'great beauty'	2	Reward clear explanation supported by actual quotations from the passage.

8.	Answers will vary. Look for interesting, insightful comments, supported by evidence from the text, which may include: • ever changing: 'restless sea' • remote: 'desolate' landscape • 'cold and sombre' • a powerful/destructive force: 'the encroaching sea'/'blackened and ruptured stone	5	Reward sensible, empathetic responses, supported by relevant evidence from the passage.
9.	Answers will vary. Reward any sensible, observant comments, supported by illustrative evidence from the passage, which may include: • 'one of the last of the wild places' • 'desolate, utterly lonely' • 'cold and sombre colour' • 'and its usefulness came to an end'	6	Reward detailed explanations with relevant quotations. Full marks for three quotations with three brief comments or two with more detailed expositions.

Exercise 1.14: *The Magical Feeling of Flying* from *Five Children and It* by E. Nesbit

Question	Answer	Mark	Additional guidance
1.	The children's wings shimmer and change colour, like the scum that floats on water.	1	
2.	According to the writer, we all know what flying feels like because we have all dreamed about flying.	2	
3.	*Answers may vary. A sample answer follows:* This statement has the effect of making the act of flying seem wondrous or magical. When we say something is 'beyond words' we mean it is indescribably beautiful or enjoyable.	3	Reward sensible, clear explanations, showing an understanding of the author's message here.
4.	*Answers will vary, and may include:* • hovering in the same place • like treading water • not moving forward but staying in the same space	2	Reward good use of own words to explain the sentence in the passage.
5.	Cyril was referring to the fact that they were all contemplating taking some of the plums from the orchard below.	3	Full marks for a clear, sensible conclusion, showing evidence of reading around the statement (i.e. the paragraph before).
6.	With wings they resemble birds and, as Jane says, no one scolds birds for stealing food.	2	One mark only for an incomplete/less clear explanation.
7.	The children saw a stout man who looked exactly like he owned the plum trees.	2	One mark for an incomplete answer.

| 8. | *Answers will vary. Look for interesting, insightful choice of words and phrases from the passage, with reasons for choice and commentaries on the words' effects.*
 Possible quotations include:
 • 'like a rainbow'
 • 'It was most wonderful and more like real magic than any wish the children had had yet.'
 • 'sailed on their great rainbow wings' | 5 | |
| 9. | *Answers will vary. Reward evidence of reading and understanding the passage, and showing empathy when writing in role.* | 6 | Reward accurate, consistent use of first person narrative and empathy. |

Exercise 1.15: *Journey Through Time* from *The Time Machine* by H. G. Wells

Question	Answer	Mark	Additional guidance
1.	The sun was 'hopping swiftly across the sky' because the time machine was racing through days, giving the impression that the sun was rising and setting within a minute.	2	
2.	The snail was the slowest thing that crawled but it appeared to dash past, too fast for the time traveller.	2	
3.	The rapid succession of darkness and light was excessively painful to the speaker's eye.	1	
4.	*Colours include:* • black • grey • blue • 'streak of fire' • brown • green	3	Three colours for three marks.
5.	'I was still on the hillside upon which this house now stands, and the shoulder rose above me grey and dim.'	2	One mark for an incomplete or less illuminating sentence.
6.	According to the speaker, the architecture of the future is great, splendid and much larger than any of the buildings which he is used to seeing.	3	Three marks for a full explanation, incorporating evidence from the text.
7.	*Answers may vary; a sample answer follows:* The sentence indicates that the hillside becomes covered in trees and plants which are a richer green in colour and seem undisturbed by the seasons. This suggests that the trees are evergreen, or that the seasons no longer change in the way they do now.	2	

| 8. | *Answers will vary. Look for references to the following evidence from the passage:*
unimpressed at first:
• 'excessively unpleasant'
• 'horrible anticipation'
• change as the experience unfolds: 'unpleasant sensations of the start were less poignant now'
• 'They merged at last into a kind of hysterical exhilaration'
becoming obsessed:
• 'with a kind of madness growing upon me'
a further change:
• 'a fresh series of impressions grew up in my mind – a certain curiosity and therewith a certain dread' | 5 | Reward clear and concise observations, backed up by pertinent quotations from the passage. |
| 9. | *Answers may vary. Look for any of the following, each backed up with evidence:*
• perceptive
• attention to detail
• sensitive to moods and atmospheres
• poetical
• brave
• eloquent | 6 | Reward any sensible, logical responses, which are supported by evidence from the passage. |

Exercise 1.16: *Coming into Play* from *Coming into Play – My Life in Test Cricket* by Andrew Strauss

Question	Answer	Mark	Additional guidance
1.	*Acceptable answers are:* • phone calls • tipped off by a journalist • via the radio or television	3	One mark per correct response. Three needed in total.
2.	Strauss found it difficult to concentrate on the game because he had just found out that he had been selected to play for England.	2	
3.	Strauss finally realised that he was in the team for real when his England kit arrived at his house.	1	
4.	*Answers will vary, and may include:* • being in an elite club of England players • being in a private world • being part of the England machine • being a member of a secret society	2	
5.	*Answers may vary. Possible responses are:* • he could not stop himself from smiling • he kept staring at them • he thought it was fantastic • he felt very proud • he felt that he had finally made it	2	Two marks for two brief comments relating to the passage, or one detailed response – using own words.
6.(a)	His parents thought that cricket was just 'a bit of fun' and was something Andrew would 'drift away from' as he got older.	2	
(b)	They thought he would get a 'job in the City' which usually means something in finance, e.g. a stock broker or banker.	1	

7.	Strauss had shown in his career to date: • tenacity/constancy: 'pleased that I had stuck at my cricket' • diligence: 'worked diligently'	2	Both points needed for full marks.
8.(a)	*Answers may vary. Suggestions follow:* • There were moments when I thought cricket was rather dull and boring. • There were occasions when cricket, for me, was monotonous and dreary.	2	Reward sentences that capture a similar meaning, but using new synonyms.
(b)	*Answers will vary. A suggestion follows:* Strauss may have found the long training sessions monotonous at times, especially in bad weather, or travelling long distances to matches.	2	
9.(a)	*Answers may vary. Accept any sensible conclusions supported by evidence from the passage. Acceptable conclusions (which require evidence) are:* • strong commitment • from a young age • unwavering • has self-belief • worth investing in	2	Comments must be supported by quotations from the passage. Fewer marks for descriptions with no evidence in support.
(b)	*Answers may vary. Possible responses (which need evidence in support) include:* • modest • feet on the ground • excitable • diligent • decisive • independent minded	4	Reward sensible comments, each one supported by a word or two from the passage, or indirect references to the passage.

Exercise 1.17: *It Shouldn't Happen to a Vet* by James Herriot

Question	Answer	Mark	Additional guidance
1.	'I had been away for only two weeks but it was enough to bring it home to me afresh that working in the high country had something for me that was missing elsewhere.'	2	One mark for incomplete quotation.
2.	*Any two of the following:* • snow: creating a 'dark trough between the snow-covered Pennines and the distant white gleam of the Hambletons…' • rain: 'in April the rain squalls drifted in slow, heavy veils across the great green and brown dappled expanse…' • fog: 'like a rippling layer of cotton wool with dark tufts of trees and hilltops pushing through here and there.'	2	Two separate descriptions for two marks.
3.(a)	*Answers will vary. Look for sensible, insightful responses which show an understanding of the shared attributes of clouds of fog and cotton wool.*	1	
(b)	*Answers will vary. Look for similes which suggest the same attributes as cotton wool/clouds of fog.*	1	
4.	*Responses may involve:* • it seemed as though there was no activity in the fields • the summer heat created a lazy atmosphere across the land • the fields looked calm and peaceful	2	
5.	He was thirteen and was reading an article about careers for boys in the Meccano Magazine.	2	
6.	Herriot had had a vision of treating people's pets in his own, hi-tech animal hospital, rather than nursing cattle on a Yorkshire hillside.	2	

7.	The author enjoys living in Yorkshire. *Possible evidence includes:* • He feels homesick when away: 'I had been away for only two weeks but it was enough to bring it home to me afresh that working in the high country had something for me that was missing elsewhere.' • Herriot enjoys spending many hours standing and staring at the Yorkshire landscape. • Herriot finds it peaceful and calm: 'and the peace which I always found in the silence and the emptiness of the moors filled me utterly.'	4	Two marks for the first explanation; two marks for one quotation in support.
8.	*Answers may vary. Suggestions follow:* • he appreciates the countryside • he enjoys spending time admiring views of Yorkshire • he enjoys peace and quiet • he is independent/enjoys his own company • he is nostalgic • he is determined	5	Full marks for detailed, insightful comments which show understanding of the passage. Five brief descriptions for full marks, or three more detailed ones.
9.	*Responses must refer to his original aims to run his own veterinary hospital and specialise in treating small animals. There should be no reference to treating cows on Yorkshire farms.*	4	Responses must be in first person, writing in role as James Herriot, and answering the question put to him.

Exercise 1.18: *A Storyteller Explains* from *Singing for Mrs Pettigrew, a Story-maker's Journey* by Michael Morpurgo

Question	Answer	Mark	Additional guidance
1.	Morpurgo was usually trying to get himself out of trouble.	1	
2.	The purpose of his explanations this time is to try to understand how and why he writes what he does.	2	
3.	*Answers will vary. One possible suggestion is:* To excuse oneself is to give an excuse for what one may or may not have done. To explain oneself is to explain how and why one behaves in a particular way.	2	
4.	*Answers may vary. A suggested response follows:* A weaver of dreams is someone who creates fictional stories and fantasies – like the dreams we imagine – for others to read and enjoy.	3	Reward clear and insightful responses, with alternative words or phrases for 'weave' and 'dream' particularly.
5.	*Any two of the following:* • parent/mother • teacher • author/writer	2	No marks for two names of writers (i.e. two different kinds of people required).
6.	*Answers will vary, and may include:* • troublesome (as a boy) • quick witted • imaginative • eloquent • reflective/thoughtful • analytical • patient • determined	3	Full marks for three separate descriptions.
7.	*Various answers are possible here. Some suggestions are:* • imaginative • resilient/determined • patient • focused • daydreamers • observant	3	Full marks for three different characteristics which writers might share.

8.	*Answers may vary. Any sensible comments will do, provided they show some understanding of – and sympathy with – Morpurgo's words in the passage.*	4	
9.	*Answers will vary. Anything well-considered and empathetic is acceptable, provided it is written in the first person, in the role of Michael Morpurgo.*	5	Reward responses that show evidence of the passage being read and understood.

Exercise 1.19: *Double Agents Wanted* from *'Why video gamers make the best spies'* from The Times, 18th October 2007

Question	Answer	Mark	Additional guidance
1.	The advertisements for new recruits will be fed into computer games. *Also accept:* – will appear on billboards in the fictional landscapes of computer games.	1	
2.	*Definitions may vary. Some suggestions are:* (a) skilled with computers; having much knowledge of computers (b) possessing technical skills (c) sharp; able to think quickly	3	One mark for each reasonable definition/synonym.
3.	*A suggestion follows:* We know that we must move with the times; we must evolve to keep pace with the changes around us.	2	Two marks for any reasonable, sensible response that accurately captures the sentiment.
4.	MI5 have advertised for staff on the sides of London buses.	1	
5.	They may be disappointed as the work involves computer programming and creating software in Cheltenham, and 'will be nowhere near any James Bond-style exploits'.	2	References to both the work type and the location are needed for full marks. One mark for referring to 'James Bond-style exploits' only.
6.	The suggestion that 'video gamers hooked on espionage-inspired adventures' could 'live out their fantasies' is misleading, as the real work does not involve any adventures at all, and is based in GCHQ in Cheltenham.	3	Reward clear, accurate explanations which refer to evidence from the whole passage.
7.	*Answers may vary. Look for:* Video gamers may be ideal candidates as they will be: • computer savvy • technologically able • quick-thinking and these skills suit the kind of work which takes place at GCHQ.	4	Full marks for identifying the skills *and* linking them to the kind of work involved.

8.	*Answers will vary. Look for references to:* • exciting opening: 'live out their fantasies' • reference to the Double Agent game • including the description of the skills needed: computer savvy...etc. • including exciting quotations from GCHQ spokesperson: e.g. 'plant the idea in the heads of young players' / 'We know we can't stand still' • use of exciting descriptive phrases: 'adrenaline-addicted video game junkies'	4	
9.	*Answers will vary. Look for, and reward, advertisements that use and apply evidence from the passage, and have clearly been written from the viewpoint of GCHQ staff.*		

Exercise 1.20: *Man's Closest Relative* from *Dawn to Dusk* by Jonathan Scott

Question	Answer	Mark	Additional guidance
1.	Scott's first encounter lived up to expectations, as he says in the passage: 'Whatever I might have expected, my first glimpse of the chimps was just as exciting as everybody had predicted it would be.'	2	One mark for answer; one mark for supporting evidence.
2.	'and my shirt was sodden from the exertion'	1	
3.	*Answers may vary; look for reference to:* • at the top of a steep hillside • at the edge of a clearing in the forest	2	Two details needed for two marks.
4.	The way in which Freud was sitting was uncanny: relaxed, one foot crossed over his leg and one arm cupped behind his head – a typically human pose.	2	
5.	According to the writer, a chimpanzee's gaze is similar to a human's because it is 'questioning, expressive and inquiring'. A chimp looks to see what you are doing, with a 'familiar knowingness'.	3	Reward clear explanations which refer to evidence in the passage.
6.	*Answers may vary. A suggestion follows:* • shone with a recognisable look of wisdom.	2	Reward original definitions which avoid repetition of key words in the question.
7.	*Answers will vary. A suggestion follows:* The author means he was thoroughly engrossed in the experience – he felt rapt and spellbound in the young chimp's company. The experience taught him how similar we humans are to chimpanzees and that we, like them, are part of the natural world.	4	Look for a clear response to both elements of the question – two marks available for each part.

8.	*Answers will vary. Look for sensible, thoughtful responses which demonstrate understanding and empathy. Any of the following references would be acceptable:* • he sees them as our equals in status and value • fascinated by them • likes to study them closely • thinks we can learn a lot from them • believes we share their natural world	4	
9.	*Answers will vary. Again, look for evidence of understanding and empathy. Reward responses that accurately postulate Scott's views (in role).*	5	

Exercise 1.21: *Because it is there* from *'We choose to go to the Moon'* speech by John F. Kennedy (12th September 1962)

Question	Answer	Mark	Additional guidance
1.	Satellites in space are helping ships at sea to find a safer course. They are also giving us advanced warnings of hurricanes and storms.	2	Two marks for two distinct ways in which satellites are helping us.
2.	The growth of science and education in America will be enriched by 'new knowledge of our universe and environment, by new techniques of learning and mapping and observation, by new tools and computers for industry, medicine, the home as well as the school...'	2	One mark for an incomplete answer. Full quotation needed for two marks.
3.(a)	1.8 million/1 800 000	1	
(b)	*Answers may vary. A possible response is:* Kennedy uses this comparison because it is widely accepted that cigarettes and cigars are detrimental to our health, and so there are far worthier things to spend money on – such as space exploration.	2	Reward clear, sensible explanations.
4.	*Possible answers are:* • a gamble • an act of trust • not knowing what will happen • a risky act	2	One suggestion with explanation or two suggestions for full marks.
5.	*Answers may include:* • makes it sound more impressive • builds drama • captures the audience's interest/attention • makes the audience more excited • makes the audience feel more inspired	3	Reward clear explanations which show empathy with audience as well as understanding of Kennedy's techniques.
6.	The next paragraph relaxes his audience and amuses them.	2	

7.	The reference to George Mallory helps to inspire the audience, as it is a tale of courage and determination. The reason 'because it is there' could equally be given for space exploration.	2	
8.	*Answers will vary. Reward good choice of quotations and clear expositions in support. Look for references to passion and persuasion, as mentioned in the question.*	6	Three marks for three quotations and three marks for three discussions.
9.	*Answers may vary. Look for the following, backed up by evidence:* • to gain support for further expenditure on space exploration • to inspire future recruits for the space programme • to win support for President Kennedy and his party • to show what Man can do • to inspire college students to reach for their dreams	4	Reward sensible theories, supported by illustrative evidence.

Exercise 1.22: *A World of Plants* from *Surviving Extremes* by Nick Middleton

Question	Answer	Mark	Additional guidance
1.	'hungry for sleep'	1	
2.	It sounds as if it is easy going because the elephants would have trodden down the path to make it easier to travel along.	2	
3.	*Answers may vary; look for reference to any of the following:* • a confusion of obstacles lying in wait to trip the unwary • roots riddled the trail • fallen branches lurked to graze my shins • whole tree trunks lay across the path • head-high creepers and vines above	2	Any two descriptions for two marks.
4.(a) (b)	The roots resembled snakes as they meandered across the path. The metaphor makes the path seem even more threatening and inhospitable to the traveller. It also links with the setting and the wildlife: i.e. the forest would have snakes in it.	2 2	Reward clear explanations that link closely to the text, and demonstrate understanding of the metaphor.
5.	• great doors slamming in the clouds • huge boulders rolling in heaven •	2	
6.	He heard the rain before it reached him; he heard the 'rumbling and tumbling' and the 'deafening crashes' and he saw 'flashes of lightening'.	2	

7.(a)	Answers may vary. Look for references to: • broken through into the centre of the dark forest • made his way into the darkest, most inhospitable place • conquered the darkness	2	
(b)	Look for: • feeling as though it had been a battle that he had eventually won. • he felt that the trek had been hard going. • he was pleased to have reached the end of a gruelling journey.	2	
8.	Answers may vary. Look for any of the following: Touch: • bumpy truck ride • without wind, not even a breeze • obstructions at my feet • scratch my face Sight: • darker • littered with leaves • there were grey-brown • roots riddled the trail, • snaking across the path • shafts of welcome sunlight • immense flashes of lightening Hearing: • saplings silently struggled • thunder that sounded like doors slamming • huge boulders rolling • deafening crashes	4	Any four descriptions and quotations needed for full marks. Look for reference to more than one sense.
9.	Answers will vary. Reward responses that can be supported by good evidence from the passage.	4	Two marks for clear, justifiable response. Two marks for evidence in support.

Exercise 1.23: *Elephant Trek* from *'Nepal: Chukka-full of charm'* from The Independent (3rd November 2007)

Question	Answer	Mark	Additional guidance
1.	Three people - the writer, the look-out boy and the driver	1	
2.	*Answers may vary; a suggestion follows:* The word 'ark' suggests that the Park has a vast range of species of animal, just like Noah's Ark in the Bible.	2	
3.	Which meanders/wriggles/twists and turns through the estate.	2	Reward answers which recognise the shape, and movement, of a snake.
4.	The elephant approaching soundlessly startled the other creatures.	1	
5.	*Answers may vary. A suggestion follows:* The author is suggesting here that the scenery is so beautiful and wild that it makes him look negatively on Britain, with its cities and man-made, twenty-first century landscape.	3	
6.	The phrase reminds us of a fork-lift truck, which is strong, sturdy and able to lift very heavy objects. The word 'tusks' sounds similar to 'truck' which makes the phrase even more effective/humorous.	2	
7.	*Answers will vary. Look for any of the following suggestions, backed up by evidence from the passage (of which there is plenty):* Before: • relaxed • contented • beautiful • calm, tranquil • melodic After: • panic-stricken • fast and furious • purposeful • exciting	3	Three good comments (with evidence) needed: two for BEFORE and one for AFTER, or vice versa.

8.	Answers may vary. Any of the following is acceptable, supported by evidence: • observant • adventurous • romantic view of life • appreciates nature / environment • dislikes twenty-first century landscapes and cities • enjoys exploring, trekking holidays • not afraid to try something new	5	Reward full, detailed responses with plenty of reference to the passage to support observations and conclusions made.
9.	Answers will vary. Look for and reward advertisements that: • mention specific details from the passage • use persuasive, descriptive language effectively (i.e. recognising the genre)	6	

Exercise 1.24: *From Fish to Frogs* from *Life on Earth* by David Attenborough

Question	Answer	Mark	Additional guidance
1.	It has a gape so wide it can engulf a young mouse.	1	
2.	*A suggested answer is:* No amphibian can be said to be fit and agile.	2	
3.(a)	The tongue is not attached to the back of the mouth, as ours is, but to the front, allowing the amphibian to stick it out it much further.	2	Very clear and detailed explanations needed for full marks.
(b)	The tongue is particularly useful because the frog is a slow-moving hunter with no neck. It can use its tongue to grasp a worm or slug, hold it using its sticky surface and then carry it bodily back to its mouth.	2	
4.	Blinking draws the eye-balls down into the skull, and, with no bones beneath the eye sockets, a bulge is then caused in the roof of the frog's mouth, which helps to push the lumps of food along to the back of the throat.	2	
5.	The exception is the capacity to blink, which helps them to keep the surface of their eyes clean and smooth when they are out of the water, and a membrane which they can draw across the front of the eyeball.	2	Again, reward lucid explanations, and references to both the blinking *and* the membrane.
6.	The tongue helps the process of swallowing by producing a lot of mucus which lubricates the food and prevents it scratching the delicate membranes of the throat.	2	
7.	The fish receive sound waves through their bodies, which are then amplified by the resonance of the gas-filled swim-bladder.	2	
8.	*Answers may vary. Any reasonable, thoughtful responses are acceptable. Look for references to their intricate designs and abilities.*	5	Reward full, detailed responses with plenty of reference to the passage to support observations and conclusions made.

9.	*Answers will vary. Look for references to the following distinguishable features:* • amphibious, so can travel on land as well as in water • extendable tongue • teeth not used for chewing, so rake food with forefeet first • blinking eyes help to swallow food • capacity to blink and use membrane to cover eyes when out of the water • have eardrums instead of absorbing sound through their bodies like fish	6	Three clear distinctions needed, with full explanations, for six marks.

Exercise 1.25: *The Road to the Pole* from *Shackleton – A Beginner's Guide* by Christopher Edge

Question	Answer	Mark	Additional guidance
1.	*Answers may vary. Look for the following effects:* • increases drama; • portrays the cold harsh, inhospitable landscape • personification to make the cold seem like an enemy; • emphasises the effects the cold can have on humans (i.e. frost 'bite').	2	
2.	The ice froze on their exposed bodies and their hooves became wounded by the jagged edges of the sastrugi ridges.	2	
3.	'By December the party had passed through Scott's furthest point south...'	2	More than the word 'Scott' needed for full marks.
4.	He named it after the man who had generously backed/sponsored/funded his expedition.	2	
5.	*Accept answers along the lines of:* • gorge • ravine • valley • chasm	2	
6.	The force of Socks's fall shattered the wooden bar that attached the pony to the sledge so, miraculously, it did not follow Socks down the crevasse.	3	Reward clear explanations which show understanding of the situation. Less marks for partial answers.
7.	*Answers may vary; a suggestion is:* • Shackleton strived to keep his men cheerful and positive	2	
8.	*Answers will vary. Look for any of the following, illustrated by evidence from the passage:* • courageous • decisive • fair • sensitive – keen to keep up morale • determined	5	

| 9. | *Answers will vary. Reward accurate and empathetic writing in role, which mentions specific details and events from the passage. Look especially for attempts to convey Shackleton's character too.* | 6 | Half a page needed for full marks. |

Part two: Composition – marking guidance

Part two: Composition – marking guidance

A marking criteria grid follows for each type of writing task. There is no mark scheme produced by the ISEB for Paper 2 at 11+, so the following are suggested frameworks only and may be departed from at readers' discretion.

MARKING CRITERIA FOR EXERCISE 2.1: Imaginative writing	
Assessment focus for imaginative writing:	Marks available: 25
Interpretation - *imaginative ideas, pertinent to chosen title, and developed throughout*	5
Language - *effective and imaginative use of literal and figurative description; exciting vocabulary, showing evidence of attempts to reach for interesting synonyms*	5
Style - *good mix of simple, compound and complex sentences to create interest and dramatic tension; use of paragraphs; effective and consistent use of first or third person narrative*	5
Accuracy and presentation - *accurate sentence construction; correct use of punctuation throughout; accurate spelling; well-presented work; legible, cursive handwriting.*	10

MARKING CRITERIA FOR EXERCISE 2.2: Personal recounts and descriptions	
Assessment focus for personal recounts and descriptions:	Marks available: 25
Interpretation - *appropriate choice of subject, relevant to title; introduced and developed without departing from central tenet of question.*	5
Language - *good use of chronological devices; effective use of creative language to create a dramatic account; accurate and consistent use of past tense and first person narrative throughout.*	5
Style - *good portrayal of personal thoughts and reflections; reactions to events rather than straight narration of them; some evidence of humour.*	5
Accuracy and presentation - *accurate sentence construction; correct use of punctuation throughout; accurate spelling; well-presented work; legible, cursive handwriting.*	10

MARKING CRITERIA FOR EXERCISE 2.3: Discursive and persuasive writing	
Assessment focus for discursive and persuasive writing:	Marks available: 25
Interpretation - *accurate grasp and expansion of central tenet of question; identifying key issues and arguments relating to topic, logical development of argument(s).*	5
Language - *good use of devices to express / switch between opinion(s); use of formal language appropriate to context and purpose; use of language to distinguish between fact/opinion.*	5
Style - *logical, progressive argument(s); relevant and focused throughout; use of illustrative evidence, use of an introduction to define terms, and a conclusion at the end.*	5
Accuracy and presentation - *accurate sentence construction; correct use of punctuation throughout; accurate spelling; well-presented work; legible, cursive handwriting.*	10

MARKING CRITERIA FOR EXERCISE 2.4: Writing about books	
Assessment focus for writing about books:	Marks available: 25
Interpretation - *accurate grasp of question and appropriate selection of text; good knowledge of text chosen; identifying key issues raised in question and discussing these in context of book(s) read.*	5
Language - *consistent use of first person narrative; good use of devices to show personal opinion and reflection; effective use of persuasive/evaluative language.*	5
Style - *evidence of good understanding of literary themes raised; logical and progressive discussion, with reasons for judgements made; introduction to set out theme(s) and conclusion at end.*	5
Accuracy and presentation - *accurate sentence construction; correct use of punctuation throughout; accurate spelling; well-presented work; legible, cursive handwriting.*	10

MARKING CRITERIA FOR EXERCISES 2.5 and 2.6: Writing about pictures	
Assessment focus for writing about books:	Marks available: 25
Interpretation - *imaginative but relevant interpretation of subject/contents; accurate and detailed observation of picture; efficient use of clues and features within picture to inform writing.*	5
Language - *effective and imaginative use of literal and figurative language to describe the subject of picture; exciting vocabulary, showing evidence of attempts to reach for interesting synonyms.*	5
Style - *consistent development of idea rising out of picture; good mix of sentence types to create interest and dramatic tension; effective and consistent use of first or third person narrative, as appropriate to choice of theme.*	5
Accuracy and presentation - *accurate sentence construction; correct use of punctuation throughout; accurate spelling; well-presented work; legible, cursive handwriting.*	10

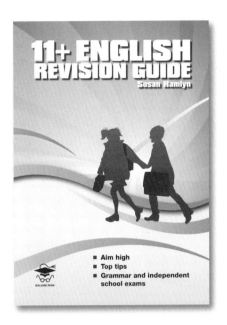

This book provides a complete mark scheme and additional guidance for *English Practice Exercises 11+* by Andrew Hammond.

Praise for English Practice Exercises 11+

'Here is a book that will stretch and stimulate pupils, and have teachers rubbing their hands with glee. A delightfully diverse selection of comprehension extracts and writing tasks to help prepare children for 11+ and beyond.'
Mike Erien, Head of English, Terra Nova School

'With this book, Andrew Hammond achieves that rare balance between providing what teachers should have and what they would enjoy teaching. This book will not gather dust from lack of use. Teachers and pupils alike will feel the benefits of Andrew's fine control of what works in the prep school classroom.'
Andrew Rose, Head of English, Cumnor House School, Sussex

About the author

After some years in the legal profession, Andrew Hammond retrained as a teacher and has taught English in prep schools for many years. He has been a class teacher, Head of English, Housemaster, Director of Studies and Deputy Head. Andrew is now Headmaster of Daneshill School, Hampshire.

Andrew has prepared boys and girls for the 11+ and 13+ Common Entrance Examinations for many years, and has served as an ISEB CE Setter and an IAPS English Subject Leader. A prolific author, Andrew has penned over thirty educational books and a five-book horror fiction series for teenagers.

Andrew is Lead Author of the Independent Curriculum, also published by Galore Park.

About Galore Park

Galore Park is the leading publisher of high quality educational resources for schools expecting rigorous academic standards, with many of the UK's top schools amongst our customers. We produce challenging books and online resources which aim high and encourage pupils to achieve to the very best of their ability. We believe that by expecting excellence, pupils can achieve excellence. To take a look at our wide range of resources for teachers, tutors and parents, please visit www.galorepark.co.uk

About ISEB

The Independent Schools Examinations Board (ISEB) offers examinations for pupils transferring from junior to independent senior schools at the ages of 11+ and 13+. The syllabuses are devised and regularly monitored by ISEB, which is composed of representatives from the Headmasters' and Headmistresses' Conference, the Girls' Schools Association and the Independent Association of Preparatory Schools.

ISBN 978-1-907047-84-8

9 781907 047848

www.galorepark.co.uk

GALORE PARK

CARRIER STRIKE

US Naval Air-Power at Sea

AIR WARS

ISBN 978-1-906959-29-6

9 781906 959296

£9.99   Printed in UK

SAM PUBLICATIONS

THE 'ESSENTIAL GUIDE' TO THE COMBAT AIRCRAFT OF THE
UNITED STATES NAVY AND MARINE CORPS

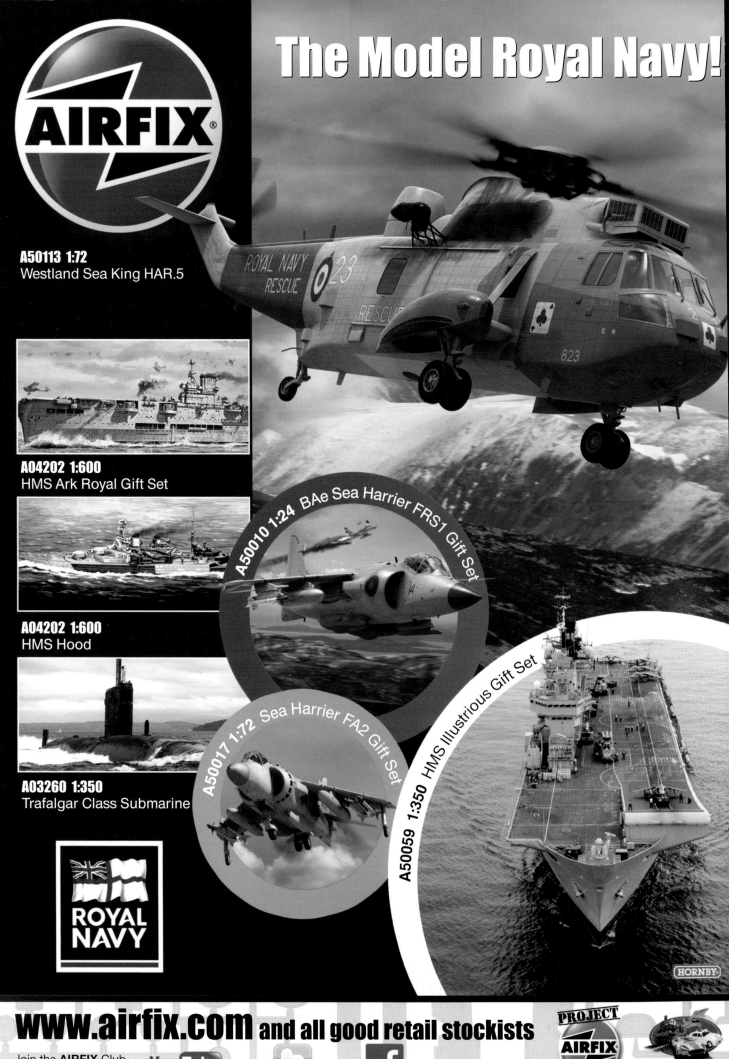